NFL's TOP 10
COACHES

by Jess Myers

NFL's
TOP TEN

SportsZone

An Imprint of Abdo Publishing
abdopublishing.com

abdopublishing.com

Published by Abdo Publishing, a division of ABDO, PO Box 398166, Minneapolis, Minnesota 55439. Copyright © 2018 by Abdo Consulting Group, Inc. International copyrights reserved in all countries. No part of this book may be reproduced in any form without written permission from the publisher. SportsZone™ is a trademark and logo of Abdo Publishing.

Printed in the United States of America, North Mankato, Minnesota
042017
092017

THIS BOOK CONTAINS
RECYCLED MATERIALS

Cover Photo: Ross D. Franklin/AP Images
Interior Photos: AP Images, 4–5, 11; John Biever/Sports Illustrated/Getty Images, 6–7; Al Messerschmidt/AP Images, 8; Ben Liebenberg/NFL Photos/AP Images, 9, 16, 23; Peter Read Miller/AP Images, 10; Ernest K. Bennett/AP Images, 12–13; Bettmann/Getty Images, 15, 20; Bruce Zake/AP Images, 16–17; Paul Spinelli/AP Images, 19; Amy Sancetta/AP Images, 20–21; Marvin E. Newman/Sports Illustrated/Getty Images, 22; Arthur Anderson/AP Images, 24–25; Chuck Solomon/AP Images, 25; David J. Phillip/AP Images, 26; Damian Strohmeyer/AP Images, 27

Editor: Patrick Donnelly
Series Designer: Craig Hinton

Publisher's Cataloging-in-Publication Data

Names: Myers, Jess, author.
Title: NFL's top ten coaches / by Jess Myers.
Description: Minneapolis, MN : Abdo Publishing, 2018. | Series: NFL's top ten |
    Includes bibliographical references and index.
Identifiers: LCCN 2016962124 | ISBN 9781532111389 (lib. bdg.) |
    ISBN 9781680789232 (ebook)
Subjects: LCSH: National Football League--Juvenile literature. | Football--
    --United States--History--Juvenile literature. | Football--United States--
    Miscellanea--Juvenile literature. | Football--United States--Statistics--Juvenile
    literature. | Football--Coaches--United States--Juvenile literature.
Classification: DDC 796.332--dc23
LC record available at http://lccn.loc.gov/2016962124

Table of
CONTENTS

Introduction

P ro football players usually go to work on Sunday. But the real work in the National Football League (NFL) happens from Monday through Saturday. That's when a team's coaching staff prepares for that week's opponent. Coaches create game plans that give their teams the best chance to win. They run practices that allow the players to put those plans into motion. And they serve as the face of the team before the media and the fans.

All of that preparation is put to the test on Sunday. For three hours, a head coach has to be aware of everything happening on the field. His duties might include substituting players, calling plays, managing the clock, dealing with the officials, and inspiring his players.

Read on for a look at the greatest coaches in the history of the NFL, and how their hard work Monday through Saturday led to glory on Sunday.

10

Bill Parcells

Bill Parcells grew up in New Jersey, playing football not far from where the New York Giants play their home games. After playing college football at Wichita State, Parcells decided to become a coach. He had stops at seven different colleges as he worked his way up the coaching ranks. Then he made the leap to the NFL, where he served as an assistant with two teams. Finally, in 1983, he was named head coach of the Giants.

His first Giants team won just three games. But the team owners had faith in Parcells, and their faith was soon rewarded. In his fourth season, Parcells led the Giants to a 14–2 record in the regular season. Then the team won its first Super Bowl title by throttling the Denver Broncos.

Parcells's coaching style focused on motivation. He was known to get inside his players' heads. He seemed to instinctively know when to scold them, when to encourage them, and when to do a mix of both.

And his players responded. Parcells and "Big Blue" got back to the Super Bowl after the 1990 season. This time they were heavy underdogs. The Buffalo Bills had an explosive offense that could score points in bunches. So Parcells drew up a game plan

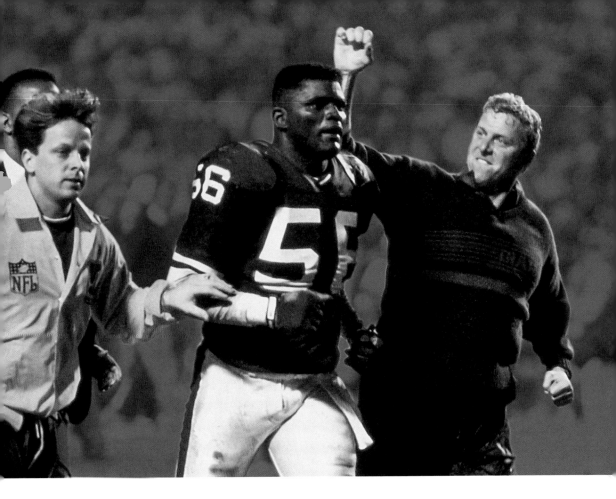

to counter Buffalo's strength. When the Giants had the ball, they focused
on their ground game. They ran the ball 39 times and kept the ball for
40:33—more than two thirds of the game. By taking time off the clock,
the Giants kept the Buffalo offense off the field. The game plan worked,
as the Giants pulled out a 20–19 upset.

Parcells would go on to coach three more teams: the New England
Patriots, the New York Jets, and the Dallas Cowboys. He took all three to
the playoffs, with the Patriots advancing to the Super Bowl and the Jets
to the conference championship game. He's the only coach in NFL history
to lead four teams to the playoffs and three of them to the conference
championship or beyond.

09

Tom Landry, *back left*, and Vince Lombardi, *front left*, cut their teeth on the Giants' coaching staff.

Tom Landry

I t has been said that football is a religion in Texas. No coach practiced that faith with more popularity over the years than Tom Landry.

Born and raised in the small town of Mission, Texas, Landry was a talented football player. His time at the University of Texas was interrupted when he went off to fly airplanes in World War II (1939–1945). After the war, he left Texas to play and coach pro football with the New York Giants.

Landry found his way back home in 1960 to coach an expansion team named the Dallas Cowboys. He would hold that job for the next 29 years. That first season was rough, as the Cowboys went 0–11–1. But Landry quickly turned the Cowboys into winners. In fact, they had a winning record every year from 1966 through 1985. No other coach in NFL history has led his team to 20 consecutive winning seasons.

From those early struggles, Landry built the Cowboys into a team so admired and successful it became known as

Landry and his trademark fedora were NFL icons for nearly 30 years.

Jim Lee Howell sure had an eye for coaching talent. When he took over the head coaching job with the New York Giants in 1954, he made two important hires. He hired Landry as defensive coordinator and Vince Lombardi to run the offense. They stayed together for five seasons and won one NFL title before Lombardi left to become a legendary coach of the Green Bay Packers.

"America's Team." Landry led the Cowboys to the Super Bowl five times and won it twice. He won 20 playoff games over his career, second most in NFL history. He retired in 1989 and was inducted into the Pro Football Hall of Fame a year later.

08

Bill Walsh

The San Francisco 49ers became a dominant team in the 1980s while relying on a system called the West Coast Offense. It's a fitting name for a game plan devised by Bill Walsh, who was a product of California from start to finish.

Born in Los Angeles but raised in the Bay Area, Walsh played college football at San Jose State. Except for a seven-season stint in Ohio with the Cincinnati Bengals, Walsh spent his entire coaching career in California. He coached at the University of California and at Stanford University. Then he jumped to the NFL, taking assistant coaching jobs with the Oakland Raiders and the San Diego Chargers. In 1979 his hard work paid off when he was named head coach of the 49ers.

Bill Walsh, *left*, and quarterback Joe Montana turned the 49ers into winners in the 1980s.

WEST COAST OFFENSE

The West Coast Offense had been around long before Walsh, but his teams made it popular. The system uses precise, short passes to move the ball down the field. That, in turn, creates more room for the ground game to pick up chunks of yards with timely runs.

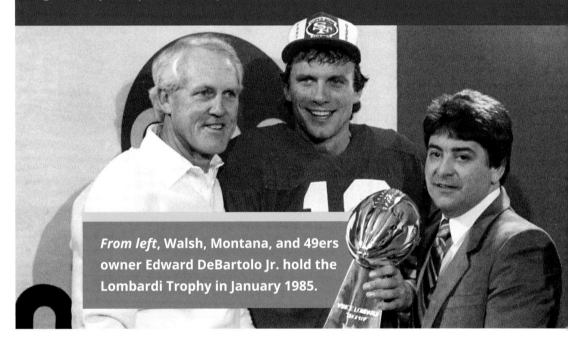

From left, Walsh, Montana, and 49ers owner Edward DeBartolo Jr. hold the Lombardi Trophy in January 1985.

The 49ers had been a mediocre team, and they won just two games in Walsh's first season. But they had drafted a quarterback named Joe Montana just before Walsh arrived. Walsh used that first season to teach Montana his preferred style of offense. It was a perfect fit. In 1981 Montana and Walsh won the first of many Super Bowls for San Francisco.

In a decade as head coach of the 49ers, Walsh's teams made the playoffs seven times and came home with the Super Bowl trophy three times. He retired from the NFL in 1989, only to return to Stanford to coach three more seasons. And the West Coast Offense is still alive and well in many teams' playbooks.

07

George "Papa Bear" Halas was the face of the Chicago Bears for five decades.

George Halas

I f you watch the Chicago Bears play, you may notice the initials "GSH" on each player's sleeve. George S. Halas died in 1983. Yet there is a good reason the Bears still honor him every time they play a game. Halas, known for decades as "Papa Bear," was the face of the Bears from the start.

Halas served his country in World War I (1914–1918) and played football at the University of Illinois. He began playing for the Decatur Staleys football team in 1920. A year later, Halas gained control of the team and moved it to Chicago. After one year as the Chicago Staleys, the team was renamed the Bears because they played at Wrigley Field, home to baseball's Cubs.

First as a player-coach and then just as a coach, Halas roamed the Bears sideline for 40 years. He suffered just six losing seasons in that time and led Chicago to six NFL championships. Halas and his teams were known for creative offense moves. His ball carriers employed spins and fakes to gain extra yards in an era when most runners plowed straight ahead.

Halas retired from coaching in 1967, but he stayed involved with the Bears until his death in 1983.

Paul Brown, *center*, was an innovator among early football coaches.

Paul Brown

Paul Brown was already a coaching legend in his home state of Ohio in 1946. He had been a star high school player, coached Massillon High School to six state championships, and had coached Ohio State to the college national title. So he was a perfect fit to run Cleveland's new pro team in the All-America Football Conference (AAFC).

The team needed a name, and some thought "Panthers" would be appropriate. But the overwhelming choice of fans and ownership was to name the team after their popular first coach. Thus, the Cleveland Browns were born.

Over the next decade, Brown would lead the team that carried his name to seven league titles. Four came in the AAFC, and three more came after the Browns joined the NFL in 1950. He brought a number of innovative ideas to the game. He was the first to hire full-time assistant coaches. He was the first to regularly study game film to evaluate his players' performance. And Brown played a role in developing the first facemasks for football helmets.

Brown left Cleveland after the 1962 season, but six years later he helped create the Cincinnati Bengals in the American Football League (AFL). He served as the new team's first coach. He retired in 1975, and he died in 1991 at the age of 82. But his legacy lives on in two Ohio cities.

Cleveland still has the Browns. And the Bengals opened a sparkling new home field on the banks of the Ohio River in 2000. It's named Paul Brown Stadium in his memory.

05

Chuck Noll

Chuck Noll was inducted into the Pro Football Hall of Fame in 1993.

The Pittsburgh Steelers and the Cleveland Browns have an intense rivalry. Part of it stems from the idea that a man from Cleveland coached the Steelers to their greatest glory. Chuck Noll was born and raised in Cleveland. He played college football at nearby Dayton University. Then he played for the Browns until he retired from the game when he was 27 years old.

After assistant coaching stints with the AFL's San Diego Chargers and NFL's Baltimore Colts, Noll got the chance to be a head coach in Pittsburgh starting in 1969. He was just 37 years old.

Noll was a fixture on the Pittsburgh sidelines for 23 seasons.

The Steelers took their lumps in Noll's first season, but their ugly 1–13 record earned them the top pick in the NFL Draft. They used it on quarterback Terry Bradshaw, who led them to four Super Bowl victories. Star running back Franco Harris and wide receivers John Stallworth and Lynn Swann played big roles, too. Noll also began building a fearsome defense that became known as the "Steel Curtain." It helped the Steelers dominate football in the 1970s. By the time that decade ended, Noll was the first coach in pro football history with four Super Bowl titles.

Noll was known for his attention to the smallest details, insisting his team play the game the right way. He would make his team practice plays over and over until they got them exactly right. He enjoyed seeing that attention to detail translate into success on the field during games. So did the army of fans clad in black and gold in western Pennsylvania and throughout the world.

Joe Gibbs is the only NFL coach to win Super Bowls with three different starting quarterbacks.

Joe Gibbs

Joe Gibbs was a star quarterback in high school in California. Then he played college football at San Diego State before beginning his climb up the coaching ladder with the San Diego Chargers. But when an opportunity to be a head coach arose in 1981, even though it was on the other side of the country, Gibbs packed his bags for Washington, DC.

The Washington Redskins had been struggling before his arrival. But Gibbs changed their fortunes in a hurry. His second season ended with the team traveling to Southern California to play in the Super Bowl. Washington beat the Miami Dolphins to win the first championship in team history.

Gibbs won three Super Bowls in his 12 years with Washington. Three different quarterbacks—Joe Theisman, Doug Williams, and Mark Rypien—led the team to NFL championships. Gibbs also found varied ways to win. His teams often relied on a huge offensive line known as "the Hogs" to protect the passer and clear the way for the ground game. Gibbs developed a reputation for finding players who had struggled elsewhere—such as Williams and running back John Riggins—and turning them into stars in Washington. He initially retired in 1992, but he returned to coaching for a second stint in Washington from 2004 to 2007.

GIBBS RACING

After his first retirement, Gibbs founded and operated Joe Gibbs Racing. It became one of the most successful organizations in motorsports, with four NASCAR championship drivers through 2016. Gibbs's son, J. D., took over leadership of the organization when Joe Gibbs returned to the NFL.

03

Don Shula is carried off the field in 1993 after breaking George Halas's record for most NFL victories by a coach.

Don Shula

Every coach works toward perfection. But only one coach in the history of pro football has ever achieved a perfect season.

In 1972 Don Shula coached the Miami Dolphins to a 14–0 record in the regular season. Then the Dolphins won two playoff games and beat Washington in the Super Bowl. That made them the first—and so far the only—team to complete an unbeaten, untied season in NFL history. But they weren't done. Even though they lost two games the next season, the Dolphins won their second straight Super Bowl title. That two-year run was the highlight of Shula's 26 seasons in Miami. It made him a legend among the fans in football-crazy South Florida.

Shula played defensive back in the NFL for seven seasons. In 1963 he was named head coach of the Baltimore Colts when he was just 33. He led

Shula had a successful run with the Baltimore Colts in the 1960s.

FAMILY TREE

Shula's two sons followed their dad in the family business. Dave Shula was a longtime NFL assistant and was the Cincinnati Bengals' head coach from 1992 to 1996. Mike Shula also is a longtime NFL assistant and was the head coach at the University of Alabama from 2003 to 2006.

the Colts to seven straight winning seasons and their first Super Bowl appearance before he left for Miami in 1970.

Shula's early Dolphins teams were known for their powerful offensive lines that cleared the way for talented running backs Larry Csonka and Mercury Morris. By the middle 1980s, when Shula brought the Dolphins back to the Super Bowl twice, he had changed his approach to fit his talent. Star quarterback Dan Marino threw touchdown passes to talented receivers such as Mark Clayton and Mark Duper at a record-setting pace. Shula retired after the 1995 season with a record 347 career regular-season and playoff victories and a legacy of perfection firmly in place.

02

Vince Lombardi was one of the truly iconic coaches in NFL history.

Vince Lombardi

Vince Lombardi made a promise to his team one cold day in 1960. His Green Bay Packers players helped him live up to it.

One year earlier, the New York native had traveled halfway across the country to the small town of Green Bay, Wisconsin, to coach the Packers. He was an immediate hit. In his second season in Green Bay, the Packers fell just short of the NFL title, losing to the Philadelphia Eagles in the NFL Championship Game. In the locker room that day, Lombardi sternly told his players that he would never again accept defeat from them on a championship stage. And Lombardi's Packers didn't lose on that stage again.

Lombardi helped turn a cold-weather outpost into Titletown.

In his nine years in Green Bay, Lombardi never suffered a losing season. The Packers' success prompted fans to start calling the community "Titletown," a nickname still used today. In all, Lombardi led the Packers to five NFL championships, including winning the first two Super Bowls, which came after the 1966 and 1967 seasons. And after that loss to the Eagles in 1960, his Packers were 9–0 in the postseason.

Whether stalking the sidelines in a trench coat and fedora or in his shirtsleeves with a tie, Lombardi was an iconic figure in the NFL. He became known for his inspirational speeches and philosophical quips. One was, "We would accomplish many more things if we did not think of them as impossible." And "The dictionary is the only place where success comes before work" was another favorite.

Lombardi left Green Bay after winning his second straight Super Bowl in January 1968. He returned to the NFL two years later to coach in Washington, but his comeback only lasted one season. Lombardi was diagnosed with cancer in 1970 and died later that summer. The NFL named the Super Bowl trophy the Vince Lombardi Trophy in his honor.

Bill Belichick, *right*, coached under Bill Parcells with the New York Giants in the 1980s. →

Bill Belichick

B ill Belichick's career is a perfect example of the power of never giving up.

Belichick grew up in a coaching family. His father, Steve, was a scout and a coach with the US Naval Academy for more than 30 years. Growing up on the East Coast, Bill was a football and lacrosse star in high school and college.

After college Belichick had a successful run as a defensive assistant for the New York Giants under Bill Parcells, helping the team win two Super Bowls. In 1991 he got his big chance to be a head coach with the Cleveland Browns. But in five seasons with Cleveland, Belichick's teams managed just one winning season. He was fired in 1995.

That's when the improbable comeback of one of the NFL's now-legendary coaches began. Belichick quickly reconnected with Parcells, serving as his assistant head coach and secondary coach for one season in New England and three seasons with the New York Jets. Belichick got a second chance to be a head coach with the New England Patriots in 2000. It started badly, with a 5–11 record in his first season. But losing seasons soon became a distant memory in New England.

Expectations plummeted when starting quarterback Drew Bledsoe was injured in the second game of the 2001 season. But Belichick had a plan. With little-known quarterback Tom Brady leading the offense, the Patriots rode a steady offense and swarming defense all the way to the Super Bowl. There, they upset the powerful St. Louis Rams on the game's final play. It was the first title for the Patriots and their coach, but it would not be the last.

The Browns weren't very successful during Belichick's five-year run in Cleveland.

Belichick is known for his no-frills style, offering very little information to the press or the fans about his tendencies. He prefers to keep that information secret, to the advantage of his team. The style works. With Belichick and Brady leading the team, the Patriots won four more Super Bowls through the 2016 season.

But their best team might have been one that didn't win it all. In 2007 the Patriots finished the regular season 16–0, becoming just the second NFL team to finish a regular season undefeated and untied. But the Patriots lost to the New York Giants in the Super Bowl, putting an unexpected blemish on an amazing season.

It was a rare loss on the big stage for Belichick, who has more playoff victories than any coach in NFL history. Belichick is known as a teacher, not only for his players but for his assistant coaches as well. More than a dozen of his assistants have gone on to be head coaches either in the NFL or in major college football. Not all of them have had immediate success. But if they learned anything from Belichick, it was to never give up, even if success doesn't come right away.

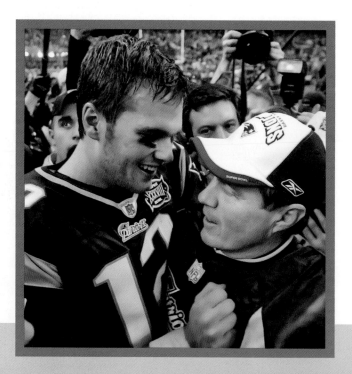

Belichick, *right*, embraces Tom Brady after the Patriots won the Super Bowl on February 1, 2004.

SPYGATE

Belichick's career in New England has included its share of controversy. In 2007 the Patriots were caught illegally filming the Jets' sideline during a game. They were accused of attempting to steal the Jets' defensive signals. The NFL fined Belichick $500,000, and the Patriots had to give up a first-round draft pick due to the so-called "Spygate" scandal.

Belichick can't believe what he's seeing in a 2016 game at New England's Gillette Stadium.

Honorable Mentions

PETE CARROLL: Sometimes, but not always, success as a pro coach is preceded by success as a college coach. Pete Carroll had to struggle as a pro coach before finding success elsewhere. After mediocre coaching stints with the New York Jets and New England Patriots, Carroll went back to college and created a dynasty at the University of Southern California. After winning a pair of national championships, Carroll returned to the NFL with the Seattle Seahawks. He is known as an innovator who earns the trust of his players. He led the Seahawks to their first Super Bowl title after the 2013 season.

TONY DUNGY: A talented quarterback in college at Minnesota, Tony Dungy earned a Super Bowl ring as a defensive player with the Pittsburgh Steelers. But his best work came on the sidelines as a head coach, first for the Tampa Bay Buccaneers and later for the Indianapolis Colts. With star quarterback Peyton Manning running the plays, the Colts won the Super Bowl in February 2007, making Dungy the first black coach to win the title. He was inducted into the Pro Football Hall of Fame in 2016.

BUD GRANT: Raised in a small town on Lake Superior, Bud Grant got used to playing outside in the cold during the long winters. As head coach of the Minnesota Vikings when they played outdoors in the 1960s and '70s, he used the cold weather as a home-field advantage. Grant's Vikings were at their best when it was below freezing outside, and Grant led the team to four appearances in the Super Bowl. A successful coach in the Canadian Football League (CFL) as well, Grant was selected for the Pro Football Hall of Fame in 1994.

JIMMY JOHNSON: After an amazing run of college success at the University of Miami, Jimmy Johnson was hired by his old college friend Jerry Jones in 1989 to resurrect the Dallas Cowboys. It was a tough go at first, but Johnson and his young team learned and grew together. By his fifth season in Dallas, Johnson had led the Cowboys to a pair of Super Bowl titles. He also coached the Miami Dolphins for four seasons and had a successful career as a TV analyst after retiring from coaching.

MARV LEVY: The Levy family came to Chicago from Canada. So it made sense that for Marv Levy's first pro football head coaching job, he'd return to Canada, where he coached the Montreal Alouettes to a pair of CFL championships. In the NFL, Levy coached in Kansas City and Buffalo and became the first coach to lead a team—the Bills—to four consecutive Super Bowl trips. The Bills went 0–4 in those title games, but Levy is remembered by Buffalo fans as a winner. He was inducted into the Pro Football Hall of Fame in 2001.

JOHN MADDEN: As head coach of the Oakland Raiders in the 1970s, Madden won an astonishing 76 percent of his games, including one Super Bowl title. The big, brash coach was loved by his players and fans. He was known as the face of the Raiders, who wear silver and black and thrive on an outlaw reputation. After stepping away from coaching, Madden gained even more fame and success as one of the NFL's top television analysts and as the man behind the popular *Madden NFL* video game series.

Glossary

coordinator
An assistant coach who is in charge of the offense or defense.

counter
Fight back against.

draft
A system that allows teams to acquire new players coming into a league.

dynasty
A team that wins multiple championships in a short period of time.

expansion team
A new team that is added to an existing league.

innovative
Having new ideas about how something can be done.

inspirational
Having the ability to influence others to want to do something.

instinctively
Based on feelings, not thoughts.

legacy
Something of importance that came from someone in the past.

motivation
A force or influence that causes someone to do something.

quip
A witty remark.

scout
A person who studies opponents in preparation for upcoming games.

For More Information

Books

Graves, Will. *NFL's Top Ten Teams*. Minneapolis, MN: Abdo Publishing, 2017.

Scheff, Matt. *Amazing NFL Stories: 12 Highlights from NFL History*. Mankato, MN: 12-Story Library, 2016.

Wilner, Barry. *Total Football*. Minneapolis, MN: Abdo Publishing, 2017.

Websites

To learn more about the NFL, visit abdobooklinks.com. These links are routinely monitored and updated to provide the most current information available.

Place to Visit

Lambeau Field

1265 Lombardi Avenue
Green Bay, Wisconsin 54304
920-569-7500
www.packers.com/lambeau-field

When it opened in 1957, the home stadium of the Green Bay Packers had seating for 32,500 fans. It's more than doubled in capacity over the past six decades and now is regarded as one of the most historic venues in professional sports. Visitors can walk through the Packers Hall of Fame, dine at an onsite restaurant, and tour the field where players still celebrate touchdowns by jumping into the arms of fans in the front row of seats—a tradition known as the "Lambeau Leap."

Index

About the Author

Originally from a small town in northern Minnesota, Jess Myers played youth and high school football and has traveled to nearly a dozen NFL stadiums around the country to attend games. Myers also writes about hockey, basketball, lacrosse, travel, politics, and the outdoors. He lives outside St. Paul, Minnesota, with his wife and three children.